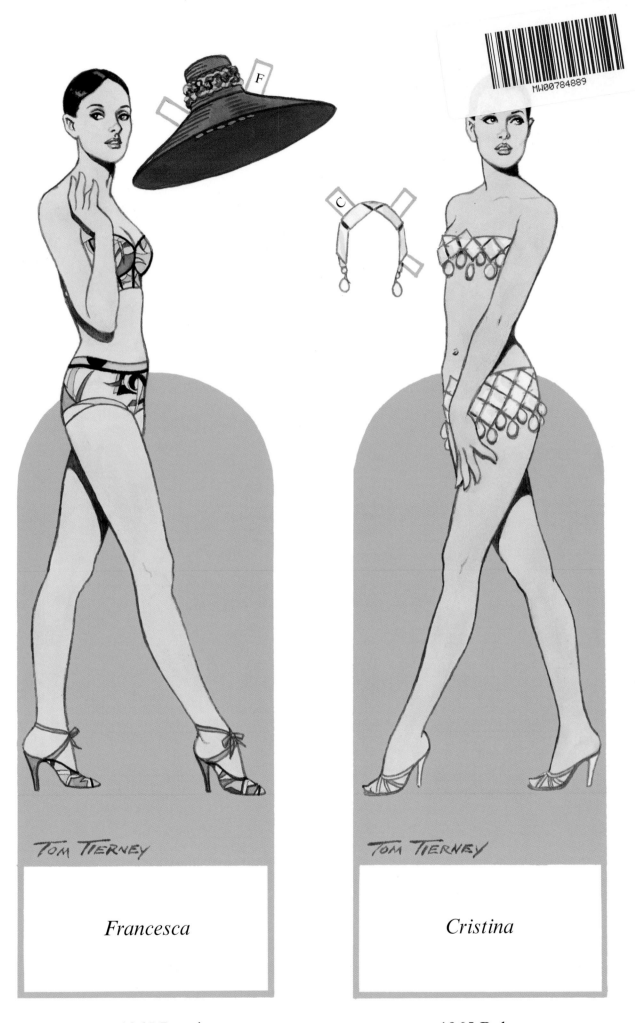

Francesca

Cristina

ca. 1965 Pucci
Bikini swimsuit

ca. 1965 Rabanne
Bikini swimsuit

PLATE 1

1950 Balenciaga
Evening gown with
feather underskirt

1988 Dominguez
Sheath dress

PLATE 2

1997 Galliano
Evening gown

ca. 1954 Pertegaz
Silk evening coat

PLATE 3

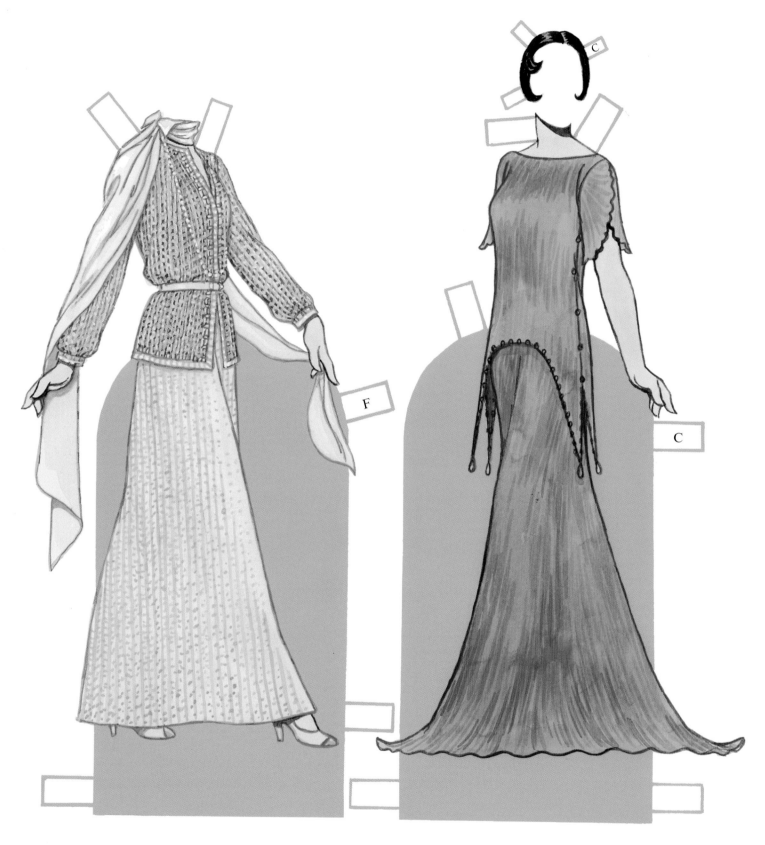

1960s Adolfo
Evening suit

ca. 1920 Fortuny
Tea gown

PLATE 4

1989 De la Renta
Ball gown

1996 Rodriguez
Silk crepe wedding dress

PLATE 5

1988 Armani
Glen plaid suit

1987 Biagiotti
Cashmere dress

PLATE 6

1985 Capucci
Taffeta ball gown

1994 Dolce and Gabbana
Leopard-print coat

PLATE 7

ca. 1997 Ferretti
Jacketed day dress

1990 Ferré
Cocktail suit

PLATE 8

1962 Sorelle Fontana
Satin dress

1992 Gigli
Earth-toned topcoat

PLATE 9

1977 Lancetti
Gilded evening dress

1986 Krizia
Unconstructed sportswear

PLATE 10

1997 MaxMara
Cashmere wrap coat

1989 Missoni
Knitwear outfit

PLATE 11

1980s Moschino
Whimsical outfit

1937 Ricci
Slimline suit

PLATE 12

1990 Sant'Angelo
Jersey bodysuit and cloak

1937 Schiaparelli
Silk crepe evening gown

PLATE 13

1955 Schuberth
Puffball evening gown

1980 Tarlazzi
Asymmetrical evening dress

PLATE 14

F

1995 Ungaro
Silk taffeta ball gown

PLATE 15

1980 Valentino
Asymmetrical cocktail dress

1991 Versace
Abstract motif evening gown

PLATE 16